flipped eye publishing

Bottle of Life

simple words, rendered sublime

Bottle of Life
flipped eye publishing
www.flippedeye.net

First Edition
Copyright © Truth Thomas, 2010
Cover Image © Menoukha Case, 2009
Cover Design © flipped eye publishing, 2010

Heartfelt thanks to the editors of the following publications in which versions of these poems have appeared:

The Houston Literary Review - *Santa Monica*
Quiddity Literary Journal - *The Gaza Strip, On Holy War, A Gerald Bird*
Little Patuxent Review - *A Lesson Before Living, A Break in the Proceedings*
Lorraine and James - *Naptural*
OVS Magazine - *Psalm for the City of Angels*
Mythium: The Journal of Contemporary Literature - *A Gerald Bird*
Naugatuck River Review - *Baltimore: Dressed in Holiday Cheer*
Pluck! - *The War is Here, Let Willie Be Willie*
Welter Literary Journal - *In Case Anyone Comes Searching*

ISBN-10: 0-9818584-2-2
ISBN-13: 978-0-9818584-2-5

Editorial work for this book was supported by the Arts Council of England

LOTTERY FUNDED

The poetry in Truth Thomas' *Bottle of Life* is intoxicatingly sweet, sharp, with a dash of bitter, good for the soul's health. I cannot think of another poet who makes me turn pages with such eagerness, to see what surprises the play of his language will bring, and what his seriously nifty wisdom will show me next. Go from a poem celebrating an inauguration in the virtual voice of Marvin Gaye, to another poem pointing out "No Afghani ever called me a nigger/ Dial down the swagger in your trigger/ finger," and you've got some heavy political meaning here too. I love this book and so will you.

—**A licia Ostriker**, author of *No Heaven*

Bottle of Life is just that, an exquisitely crafted urn that holds within the beautiful struggle that each of us experiences differently. As artist, Thomas unifies our varied journeys under the banners of pain, happiness, memory, heart and joy—all the while directing words, only as a true poet can, to resonate, provoke, and reassure.

– **Felicia Pride**, author of *The Message*

Like Etheridge Knight, Lucille Clifton and Rita Dove, Truth Thomas is a brilliant chronicler of the atrocities of our violent, "soiled world." Whether writing about theIsraeli-Palestinian conflict, a bombing in Iraq, death on the playgrounds, shots fired in New Orleans, the Crips and Bloods, a family member sentenced to the hell of prison life, or a friend dying in a nursing home, Truth Thomas shakes us from complacency with startling images and a voice that can't be ignored. He is a spiritual poet who can find heaven in his Mama's macaroni and cheese or Chuck Brown's "bustin' loose," or in the embrace of two lovers. He makes us believe that the armless can lift barbells. *Bottle of Love* is one hell of a book.

—**Jeff Friedman**, author of *Black Threads*

This is the language of collard greens and black-eyed peas seasoned with fatback and Big Mama's sweet tea. From Tennessee to the Gaza Strip, Truth Thomas' genius lies in his ability to take us places where we've never been before. Each page is like plucking the strings of a bass guitar, but the beat never gets too heavy, the message is always clear, the craft exquisite and masterful.

—**Randall Horton**, author of *The Lingua Franca of Ninth Street*

For all those born beneath an angry star
Lest we forget how fragile we are...

– Sting

Bottle of Life

For Carridella Macklin Thomas

Contents

Up Growing 13
Let Willie be Willie 18
The War is Here 20
Wade in the Water 21
For It to Take Your Head Off 22
Art 23
A Lesson Before Living 24
The Greatest Show on Earth 25
Some are Made Mechanics 26
In Case Anyone Comes Searching 27
Obamacology 28
Ode to the Iraqi Reporter who Threw His Shoes at President Bush 29
Taxi Standing 30
Love Poem to a Lesbian 31
Los Salseros 32
Davidsonville: Thanksgiving 33
Naptural 34
The Fiction Section 35
I Want You Back 36
The Great Entertainer 37
A Break in the Proceedings 39
When Mama Does the Cooking 40
¡Azúcar! 41
A Gerald Bird 42
Baltimore: Dressed in Holiday Cheer 43

A Dynamite Player 44
Playground Rules 46
Villain "L" 47
The Gaza Strip 48
On Holy War 49
Neda Soltani 50
Poem for Soldier 51
Big World 52
Night in Topeka 53
Santa Monica 54
Psalm for the City of Angels 55
We Won't Bow Down 56
Halley's Rock 57
Straight Outta Compton 58
Mailbox Confessions 59
Mirror in the Man 60
Names, Numbers, Cages 61
Roller Coaster of Love 62
On Fishing 65
Summertime and the Living is DC 66
Entitlement 67
The Holocaust Museum: June 10, 2009 68
Epitaph for All 70
Rubber Side Up 71
Manor Care Midnight 75

Up Growing

No tooth
was ever chipped
for calling a motherfucker
a "motherfucker" on a dare.
This never happened
in Takoma Park in1969
when I was ten.
No squirrels
dropped nuts
to bear witness.
No White Oaks
bent down leaves
to see this fight
at 7600 Maple Avenue
a week after we moved
into Park Ritchie—
No lip was ever split
when a boy flexed
Three Musketeer
to claim the
Afro Sheen affections
of a girl named
Almeda Bacon.
This never went down
seven days after I
elevated up to 1801,
along with my mother,
one Tennessee transplanted
sacred black sofa,
and my stepfather:

The Jolly Green Negro.
In fact, in "one small
step for man" days,
in Jackson 5, "ABC,"
"Stop the Love you Save"
days, there were no fights,
no duels in bruises.
No stepfathers
ever broke
faces of door frames
to lattice boys in
choke hungry fingers.
No one studied war then.
No battles bled.
A half a million tons
of bombs never bounced
Betty-like
on to rice-soaked earth.
Never did a Vietnamese girl
run crying in napalm skin—
not then,
or three years later
on the cover of Time.
Never did a Knoxville,
take-no-shit woman,
scratch the mug
of a 6-foot
cheating husband,
and never
did this wannabe Shaft,
wannabe man,
wrestle a woman

to the ground—not yesterme,
yesteryou, not yesterday—
not on streets where boys
would shadow box
like Muhammad Ali,
and spin,
and shuffle
and float over
girls with names like
Alice Haxton,
or Teresa Youngblood.
And no young bloods
ever woke up,
wood of erections,
like Hank Aaron
waking up home runs.
There were no erections in 1969,
no cool Hefner
no Playboy after dark
no pinball flippers
or bomb alarm drills
("This is a test, this is only a test")
no fear of nuclear strikes
(then as now).
What there was
was "Nina, Gifted and Black,"
and Sly and Stone and
"Stand" and all were
"Superbad," but no one
dared say so.
My elder sister
may have known why

caged flight sings,
but she never
wrote it down.
Black feeling,
Black Nikki,
Black talking,
was nowhere
to be found —
not "right on,"
not "solid,"
not "Everything is everything."
Cause everything was never
everything, like white
was never seen
as right (now as then).
What we was
was NBC glued
to "Julia" Tuesdays
and Flip Wilson
when he attacked us
with laughs
every Thursday night.
But the Devil
never made him do it —
him or Geraldine.
The Devil did not exist.
Violence did not exist —
not one year past U Street's
blaze and broken teeth —
not the year that Hendrix
fired up Woodstock,
burned a Stratocaster up

like a joint.
Assassinations did not exist.
Riots did not exist.
Army boot wearing,
Denture Cream pressing,
fake-ass Black Panther
abusers of women,
did not exist—and none
ever filled our apartment
with spit, and heaves,
harvests of harm.
No—none of this
ever happened—much
like games of
"hide and go get it"
I never played in woods
or ice cream trucks
I never chased
with Leroy Jenkins
and Ricky Burrell
or chewing gum cigarettes
I never bought
at Maple Avenue Deli
or prayers
I never prayed
almost every night
for my stepfather to
fall
from any window
way up high.

Let Willie be Willie

(after Johnny Lang)

Nothing startles now—
not coffins born of swine,
or newborns, dumpster sown—
not powder burns in Teddy Bears
from daddies missing paper.
"They wouldn't let Willie be Willie,"
his note read."Decapitated hope,"
it said, while hearses snake
and grave stones bare their teeth.
Nothing startles now—
not suitcase silenced lambs,
or water boarding eagles.
"If they're nude with a hood,
a little torture is good,"
cause we've got to let Willie
be Willie," old Dick says—
I mean, old Pinochet says—
I mean, old Michael Corelone says.
"We gained valuable information
in our discussions with Fredo,"
old Condoleezza says, as she
row, row, rows the boat—tows
the lie, while bulls run grocery
stores, and snowballs trigger
handguns, and high school teens
craft shrapnel rain for teachers.
Nothing startles now—only
tulips break the trance, or
(possibly) ice cream chilling
chins, or sweet propeller hands

seizing double-dutching days.
Only playground faces give
one pause—that any good
thing can still rise up, and
spring, and fall, and spring.

The War is Here

No Afghani ever called me a nigger.
Dial down the swagger in your trigger
finger. The war is here—not over hills,
everywhere. Shots fired in New Orleans,
a community down, please respond. Shots
fired in Bodymore, the unwired down.
Please respond, Mr. President. Flesh
that looks like your flesh—here. Jornaleros
used and tossed away like bottles—flesh
that looks like ours, nodding and rotting
by roadways. Shots fired, Crips, Bloods,
MS 13 down. Shots fired, Cartels, Aryan
Brotherhood, up and coming, Gallant
Knights insane. Repeat: insane days
and nights—right here. Little girls who
could be your girls, selling for a dollar in
Harlem, in Chinatown—right now—right
down the street from your 1600 dome.
No Afghani ever called me a nigger.
The war of the world is at home.

Wade in the Water

Tonight we savor the lake, hands meet,
warm as kissing pillows. Tonight we

make a wave out of no wave, as cicadas
shake their tambourines, smiles stick

on faces—sap of human being trees.
There are touches as committed as fire

in lightning flies, touches as consistent
as black upon the sky. And it is well

with our souls to anchor our hips, under
anointing of summer winking moon—

well without robes to dip into shivers,
where ninety-nine and a half won't do.

For It to Take Your Head Off

There has to be some bruise in the bed,
some lava on the backside, some callus
that rises from tattered chairs, toes
peeking through shotgun socks, maybe
ten souls in a tin shack, who cannot
keep their cool in August, or melt a cube
of ice when snowflakes come to call.
Belly full, brings nothing, and I wish
it wasn't so, for sake of son, mango life,
wife—but I didn't make these rules—
set this billiard ball in clouds. Barbells
must be lifted by the armless, legs must
be broken when they are well, blisters
are the only midwives who can guide it
from the inside screaming out.

Art

Can hook like heroin.
A radio left on
while

Coltrane plays—an
open gallery door
where

Basquiat frames—
just a little noise
and funk

under Savion's shoes
might be enough
to do it—

make you sell your house,
your car, your drawers,
for a

perfect fix
of beauty.

A Lesson Before Living

We are not grasshoppers, with legs tied in
this race, nor are our paths pinned down by rails,
reinforced with concrete, gravity's slaves.
No metal womb delivers us howling
to storefront hands, isotropic etchings,
gladiator cogs, sprockets made for sale.
We are not one-way streets in a cheese chase,
tape-measured blocks for tape-measured living.
You can turn around on this track, cross lanes
of order, scald the bitch of clicks. You can,
if you wish, sabotage the reindeer games
of men, bypass the cup of other's plans,
defy the office gangs—doors wearing names.
What one size fits all born to slip-slide shoes?
Once the gun sounds, the course is up to you.

The Greatest Show on Earth

A tiger's rich fidelity
is most often
wed to whips,
every trainer—
every woman finds,
but when a big cat
starts to wander off
at the circus,
a golf club
has been known
to change his mind.

Some are Made Mechanics

(4 Janusz Wasicki)

There are men like days—some
men, like New Year's Eve,
who summon songs to gather,
and beckon hugs to
lace the backs of strangers
of strangers. They are found
in bars and courtrooms.
Some are made mechanics,
priests. They are tall men,
and they are not. Some are
twins, and some are separate
as poles. But all of them
are built to see the better
us unknown. I raise a glass
to them, to celebrate me home.

In Case Anyone Comes Searching

The day they swore Obama in,
Marvin Gaye's suit broke out
of its case at the Hard Rock Café
and sang the National Anthem

on U Street—or was it "Pride
and Joy" on Independence Ave—
or was it "Can I Get a Witness"
on the White House lawn?

Memories fade, but I will say,
arms were goalposts, high and
toasting then, DC grew warm
as a bottle of Sake and filled up

cups, both black folks and
white folks gulped down giggles,
tears, glee, and one of those
people, grandchildren—one

of those people was me.

Obamacology

Sweet dreams are made of these: smooth chestnuts
on a once
white table
in your house—
now mine
inauguration
double double
deuce deuce
the first.
And what
did we call them?
Down payment
on a blood stained dream?
And what did
destiny's children sing?
At Last?
Sweet dreams are made of these—chestnut smooth.

Ode to the Iraqi Reporter who Threw His Shoes at President Bush

Your wingtips flew—
> two Satchel Page bullets

two major league gems
> size ten—one ball tossed

for flags waving murder
> another, for trading

> Sammy Sosa.

Taxi Standing

Whoever hails a   cab
robed in mela-   nin
whether in Brook-   lyn
or Washing-   ton
or Lon-   don
will likely be a good while   wait-
ing and pac-   ing
and swear-   ing
at every foolish   hand
that stamps us   "post
black,"   and
come to see our neon   ink
is not   that,
is left   back
is under   attack,
and it's matter of   fact,
as long   as
the canon—   white
cabbie of   barons—
drives by   colors.

Love Poem to a Lesbian

(4 Venus Thrash)

If you can only feel me for five percent
of the time, then let that five be warm as
ovens birthing bread. Let this man's kisses
climb heights of cheekbones, lips rest upon
native summits therein. Let fingers walk
tummies down, through doors of life,
to toes. Let the foot rubs say, "Amen."
Let my five percent be free to call you
nothing like a dike, or ditch, or any
charging, stabbing, thing. Let me dream
I am the pie unsliced—like you, one
hundred percent of something, speaking,
veined—like you, complete and whole,
a human being named.

Los Salseros

When smalls of backs call tips of fingers,
there is a meeting, like tattoo arms to ink,
leaves of grass to green, so that even when
music stops, there is tint of memory that
lingers (Tito Puente, Tito Rodriguez), from
pavilions of beats that steam (Willy Colon,
Hector Lavoe). This is the ballroom's
spinning remembrance. These are the updrafts
over rivers that carry us. How cinnamon
are your eyes. Tonight, is a very good night
to die.

Davidsonville: Thanksgiving

Black Turkey Buzzards dine
  beside the gray roadway, wait

for me to pass, before they
  say their grace.

Naptural

Conk my soul CJ—
lie or no lye, iron me
dark and lovely.

Fry my esteem—
burn it bone straight
100 years long.

Madam, relax me,
Creamy Crack me.
I will still be tense.

I will still be fake,
as a rain dance
in New Orleans
after a storm.

A rusting tug boat of a man, in Martin Luther King, Jr.
Memorial Library, helps an even rustier old man with
broken rudder legs, inch his way to an exit at 8:45 pm
on January 25th, 2010. The more weather worn of the two
pitches and rolls as he walks, and says, "I have no words
to express my debt for your assistance, other than to give
you my thanks," and this he continues to say: "Thank you,"
"Thank you," "Thank you," as if it were a "Mayday" call.

As they tugboat over to the guard desk, fifteen minutes
before the building chains its grill, the library is no longer
a library, but an ocean, with angry 30 foot swells. Books
are no longer books, but buoys—florescent lights, seagulls
flying. As men become ships—harbor hungry—passing
Melville, fifteen minutes before G Street sidewalk signals
them home, two vessels head for port, blankets, hot
chocolate, content to leave the monster fish alone.

I Want You Back

Though some may place a kingly sheen,
black pearl glow, on moonwalk shoes,

what hubris lies in critic's pens and moods.
No eagle loses feathers over words.

When tame, or wild, did any Motown bird
ever billboard cling, or sing his moves

as thrilling? Trash diggers will always tear
apart, but even as they attack, legend keeps

a light on for the genius child, "Billie Jean,"
and brother, I want you back.

The Great Entertainer
(4 Athar Habib)

He could peddle the Pacific Vortex,
helmet Mohawks in the red. He could
be from Pakistan, or Flushing, Queens,
or Maryland. He could be obsessive
obsessive, with challenges challenges.
Who can say? Who has ears to listen?
And what would it matter, now that we
have walled him in a cell of fame? "If
you build it, they will come." If you
ride it—1 and 39,000 miles ("one and
three nine zero zero zero miles," he says
and must repeat) in a small town, they
will call you news—ink of human
interest. This is what we call "The
Columbia Bike Guy," our knight from
Section 8 Section 8, who jousts with
highway dragons. Who cares if he
beats his body to slay the voices in
his head—their mouths run-on like
a purse snatcher in a New York subway.
No, don't tell me. Don't tell us, because
all that counts is smiles that fill his
hands when we honk to him and he
answers. He comforts us like layer
cake, the great entertainer. This is
all we want to know under the big top—
all we choose to feel. We will write
him into novel, shoot him into film.

We will cotton him a T-Shirt, call him
"Forest Gump of Spokes," sell his
decal for a dollar, press his signature
in soap, but we will never call him by
his name, for men with names may
sometimes dream of sleigh rides under
truck tires, sometimes ask how "suicide"
is spelled in May.

A Break in the Proceedings

You tornado   up
stalk red-eye the   tenure
track rainbow,   fly off
like Dorothy to Kans-   as
then crash-   land.
Your welcome   comes
from no apparent   witches—
at least you recog-   nize none.
All grins are enchant-   ing.
But something alarms   you
like fire would a scare-   crow
or rust might a tin-   man
or polygraph   tests
do the li-   ar.
You tell the Wiz-   ard
and the May-   or
and the Lolli-   pop
Guild that your   dreams
are yellow brick   roads,
wet with   thoughts
of working in the   middle
of no-   where.
How surprised you   are
to learn that not even   Toto
believes this   shit.

When Mama Does the Cooking

Macaroni & Cheese is more than a side,
more than a culinary foil, sidekick to Lake Trout,
Fried Chicken or Chicken Fried Steak, more
than a static character on kitchen counter stage,
understudy to collard greens, sweet potato pie,
or pineapple cake. It is—and I will say it—
the Holy Ghost in a pan, a taste bud tent revival,
Sweet Honey in the Rock spanking sékerés,
a seven day kiss on a plate, and at M & J's
Soul Food Restaurant on East 25th Street
in Baltimore, at four o'clock today, it was gone
in sixty seconds, and I was happy to be the one
to race it from the Christmas tree of my fork
to the finish line—winner's circle—of my face.

¡Azúcar!

Mother called them "goosebumps,"
but I know them now as "piel de
gallina," born of your billowing soul,
your ruffled trains of rumba rolling,
bata Cubana, Queen of Quimbara,
let the walls and halls and house of
salsa bow down when history calls
your name. Oh Celia! Bridge to
Africa, bridge to Cuba, can you
see these children—bridge to this
Miami night? Right now, a little girl
is singing "Tu Voz," a broomstick
doubling as a mic, her kindergarten
brother, bringing in rhythm on forks,
spoons, pots, pans—the first timbales.
See her Barbie Doll, Nichelle—fly,
in crinkle chiffon sash, conductor
of the action figure Fania All Stars.
See the "Man of Steel" revealed as
Johnny Pacheco, Batman unmasked
on bass, swaying over a sweat soaked
utility belt. See Spiderman, Green
Goblin, two-stepping with their horns,
all warring traded in for trumpets,
sugar sprinkled saxes. See Wonder
Woman missing. No, she is there.
She has always been there—la negra
tiene tumbao. She has always been
you.

A Gerald Bird

One day I will feather wings, and clap air
as he does, and he always does, ditch this
beautiful filthy perch, and glide into dance
for no particular reason. Maybe, when I see
my gray nest days, I will tap dance clouds
and electric slide in song with charm Caruso
never knew, as the Gerald Bird does—and
he always does now, carousel his by and by
days. Maybe, over a buffet table in Rome
you will find him, sharing half a sandwich
with a hungry alley cat. Maybe, you will
spot him offering sprinting tips to a squirrel,
or maybe you will hear him going on about
the owner of a New York Deli who was
murdered, but who, according to Gerald
 continued to make good pastrami sandwiches
nonetheless. Yes, one day I will glide, climb,
samba curtains of dawn, for no particular
reason. One day, I will laugh in the face
of all the horror here—all the prune drawn
bellies, all the crowbars cracking cabbages
for coins, all the shrapnel stabbing streets,
and televised gasps of grief from mothers
rocking bones, but it will not be today.
Today, there is too much blood in my eyes
to fly.

Baltimore: Dressed in Holiday Cheer

Walking on Saratoga Street, a gun barrel stops
and asks me for a smoke, and all my money.
Silver bells, silver bells, it's Christmas

time in the city... My fingers fumble through lent
like quicksand in my pockets. Outside my
body, I watch as Andrew Jackson unfolds

in my hand, and rises like Superman's cape. *City*
sidewalks, busy sidewalks, dressed in holiday
*style...*As three windows in King Tut Jewelers

keep watch by night, the handgun flies away,
a trash truck passes, and you ask me, "What
do I recall?" *Children laughing, people*

passing, meeting smile after smile, in the air
there's a feeling of... I remember night
became day, an empty box of

Ramses shivering with me on the
pavement, and hope is never
feathered in the city.

Italicized text adapted from "Silver Bells" lyric
by Jay Livingston and Ray Evans.

A Dynamite Player

Tony was a
dynamite player
blew an alto to bits—
hit notes Bird
forgot to play
or missed—lit
bebop fuses over
P-Funk cakes
spooned women
like Chinese food,
would feast
and be hungry
an hour later.
Yes, Tony was
a dynamite player—
had a dynamite gig
left Philly stages
smoking—was
an equal opportunity
fiend—was
every jones like
Chaka Khan was
every woman, and
I wanted to be him—
from his Pork Pie
to his sleep-deprived

keys—'til he
fell asleep
in a crack pipe
and burned
all the way down
to his reeds.

Playground Rules

Bully learns karma
  after school and a blizzard —
rock in a snowball.

"The boy had been missing since [Jennifer] Hudson's mother and brother were found shot to death Friday..." October 28, 2008 --Chicago Sun Times Staff Reporters

Villain "L"

(4 Julian King)

Shift happens—towers, smoke. You slip away
and leave no fingerprints, but stains of fear—
no witness to match mug shots to your wake.

Shift happens—Mumbai, ashes. Your fire rain
dances, and you don darkness, prowling years—
a shape-shifting dog, a cross-dressing snake.

What do they call you? Unknown assailant?
Dahmer? Bundy, when the bodies appear?
You are the great forger of other's names

costumed in shadows, addicted to fame.
You shush the babies so parents won't hear
your sounds of abuse, your accents of pain.

Gunshots steal a child, a city is slain.
A mother, an aunt, track serial tears.
Your pawns leave the board, take the rap in chains.

But I know it's you in gunpowder bathed.
I know it's you, both pit and puppeteer.
There is no disguising a coward's gate.
How does it feel to clean the loser's plate?

The Gaza Strip

It almost sounds like
a pole dancer's habit,

or a street in Vegas
paved with Blackjack

tables and gin. I wonder
how one colors up after

a bomb blast, or if any
know the true count,

where the house of
death always wins.

On Holy War

How fragile is the paper-mâché of flesh, and
quiet are skulls that litter the ground. I pass

your party after most of the guests have gone.
A headless boy stops and asks me if he's an

Israeli or a Palestinian's son, and which of
the bullets that struck him, was the holy one.

Neda Soltani

(1982 - 2009)

Imagine we're whales being chased by Japanese hunting
ships in rolling Ross Seas, and harpoons have landed.
We must not cower upon the hook now, as blow holes
spray briny currents red. We must fix our eyes like
hooks upon our captor captains—face death awake.
Now, more than at any other time, we must bellow
claims to waves, wave farewells to gulls, even
if they beg us not to go. We must tell them to
keep flying, focus forward, bear witness of this...

*Say my name, say my name, when no one is
around you, say "baby I love you," say my
name, say my name,* for memory is oxygen—
forgetfullness, the suffocating storm. Say
Malcolm, say Martin. Say Emmett, Medgar,
Ghandi. Say Biko, Chaney, Goodman,
Schwerner, John. Say Bobby, Addie Mae,
Cynthia, Carole, Denise. Say Neda,
we remember you. Say this.

*Italicized text from "Say My Name" lyric
by Rodney Jerkins, popularized by Destiny's Child.*

Poem for Soldier

(4 Jay Fair)

I will not sing songs
of upheld signs,
whether raised in
"Love or Leave It" crowds,
or speakers chanting
roots rock peaceful shows.
Now is not
the preaching hour,
amid pulpit sips
of Perrier—
not when it's you—
my all of you—there.
For that sandbox
filled with mortars,
your sauna
sweating rounds,
will I only sing
of planes homecoming,
boots on bases safe,
of two legs
stepping strong,
minds gripping calm
like pollen gripping bees.
Of this, and this alone,
will I take requests,
strum this old guitar.
Play I some tunes
of long life
stealing home,
or play I silence,
'til reunion comes.

Big World

Away from feral fixtures of cities,
bipolar streets, alleyways of semen
rats, piss, squirming apples, wormy
with murdering and shit, there lives
another world, they say—a world
where shade trees stand like bedposts,
grass is goose down pillows, quiet time
is not a hostage robbers hold at bay.
I run for this, like a woman's touch
after jailbreak.

Night in Topeka

No muted
trumpet
are you,
nor ever
were your
touches
gloved,
your
grooves
outside
the pocket.
Solos—
so high
you make me—
happy,
as a pillar
in the
flatlands.

Santa Monica

I breathe her, wet & silver, saint & lover
as seagulls kite, on invisible strings
catching fries. I taste her, in a funnel cake
while arcades wade on wooden legs, over
moon enraptured tide. I greet her, arch
& altar, bounce & bubble, where popcorn
plays percussion—pier draws rods like
drunken men draw trouble. Where candy
cane lights watch rails for kisses, they are
never disappointed. Where carousel horses
court laughing hands of children, I am
never disappointed. Below the ocean road
Monica reminds me, I am one of them.

Psalm for the City of Angels

(4 Land and Sheryl Richards)

In thee, O Lord, do I put my trust,
and thank you for Fat Burgers,
In-N-Out Burgers, Roscoe's Chicken
and Waffles, El Pollo Loco, Love,
Peace, and Soooooul Train, back
in the day, for record deals that came
and left like shave ice on the tongue
of the sun, for Locking, Popping,
Clowning, Krumping, roller skating
bikinis on Venice Beach (Hallelujah),
for not getting shot by LAPD for
breathing while black in Beverly
Hills (or Baldwin Hills, or Woodland
Hills, or anywhere in Los Angeles
County). I thank you, O Lord, for
"Joe's BBQ and Peach Cobbler"
(that used to be right off Crenshaw),
and Darrell Alston (with piano
fingers), who first turned me on to Joe's.
I thank you, O Lord, for flame-painted
purple Impalas, bouncing down
Hollywood nights, for Stylesville
Barbershop in Pacoima, Englewood,
Compton, Long Beach, Watts, Magic's
no-look passes at the Forum in days
of his prime, for surviving sweets
without a jimmy when I lost my mind,
and gang truces, however long they last.

We Won't Bow Down

(after AZ, NO, & WG)

As I was profiled on a ribbon of highway
I saw above me, a billy club skyway.
I saw below me, bloody feathers of
a Phoenix. This land was made for you
and we   won't bow down—not on
this ground—not Choctaw, not Chickasaw—
not Seminole, Yaqui, latino. A slave
broth boils, born of devil sun rocks—
a "Mississippi Goddamn" soup. But we
won't bow down, be gagged, be bound
to "separate but equal" place settings—
no nos doblaremos abajo—not Cherokee,
not Navajo, not all nations, africano.
Hooded cooks strain to force feed us
this pot, foul with fat of Apartheid.
Pero comeremos de la olla—not on
this ground—Grant's sparking sands of
tears and tombstone flocks. As I was
beaten on a ribbon of highway, ancestors
called me to a vision in the skyway, and
all around me, I heard them singing
"This land was made for you and we..."
won't bow down—not on this ground
of deported American eagles. This land
is your land, this land is my land, desde
California, to the whitewashed murals,
from New Orleans masking, to our ballots
dancing, this land was made for you
y para mí.

Halley's Rock

I take your hand, race ribs of Griffith Park Observatory.
Numbers tell the tale: 1986. Twenty-something-something.
We bound for what we do not know, as lovers 75 years ago,

who sleep now, did—as lovers 75 years from rising will,
to seek what youth demands—to see the new—or more
likely, for something wise to circle back and catch a view

of us—for it to see no sarcophagus of extinction has tucked
us in with dinosaur remains—for it to see, at least for one
more hour, no atom's match has wrapped our globe to

spacious skies of ash. I take your cherry hand, race ribs of
Griffith Park Observatory night, and there is no white flash,
no hypocenter wasteland, or skin that melts, or eyes that boil—

burst—on grills of mushroom clouds. There is only a line
to inch and worm through—the lone hazard—a misstep
from the queue, before we tickle a telescope's side. It will

only host his cosmic visit for us once—and this we know,
like soon we'll know his bottle rocket blinking. I smile, when
I have seen it. We smile and fly to know we have been seen.

Straight Outta Compton

Bullets jump from guns
    splashing into pools of flesh.
Crips turn into Bloods.

Mailbox Confessions

If I knew where I was going, I would send myself a postcard
certified
       dap
       first
       class
certified
four
corner
       kiss
       certified
I would send myself a postcard, if I knew where I was going

and try
       to act surprised
              the day it comes…

Mirror in the Man

I'm pocket sifting pennies, mining
sofa folds for coins. I find a photo
of a slimmer self, wealthy eyes
of a dreamer, a look of armor-plated
will, before record sales, losses —

before family ties, bosses. Normal
is a high wire. I have given bits of skin
away to balance, and still I come up
empty. But is it not the duty of
a man, to abandon artful pans after

many years of sifting? My life is
dry as dunes now. I hold the photo
up to the mirror. It takes a minute
for him to see me. We both shake
our heads, cry ourselves awake.

Names, Numbers, Cages

If he's still in the bottle, he's seen as
dragging bottom—this not so artful
dodger, this ex-communicated cousin,
who is caged in steel and stink now.
At family get-togethers, he only lives
in whispers, when aunts and uncles
shake their heads, cast their voices low.
At his first bid, he was yet a young'un,
when we would run, press miles to tires
to see him. But those were days that
passed as fast as contact visit hugs.
After triune strikes, recidivism years,
no one is sprinting down his road.
He's been playing tag with Satan,
and he won't be robbed of this game.
But, I will see him today, because it's
Christmas, and no one else will come.
I will pass through metal detector jaws,
feel jagged stares of razor wire (as he
will), be seen as walking contraband
(as he is), annul my pockets of coins,
keys, hope, lift knuckles up to Plexiglas,
hoist hellos up to phones. And, as always,
I will not ask him about clothes washed
in toilets, or shanks, or rape, or release
dates. He will not ask me about goat
curry, or pone, at the family picnic, or
if his father ever forgave him, before
he passed away.

Roller Coaster of Love

We are all strapped in past points of
"no going back," from moments
wombs welcome us to days. As I
wait on the runway of a roller coaster

with my older brother Andre, I am
reminded of this, although I cannot
help but wonder if this ride they call
Kingda Ka, here at Six Flags, means

"Scared shitless" in another time and
tongue. But, can a man say "scared"
in a poem? Even when zero becomes
128 miles an hour in 3.5 seconds,

and a hot dog is poised to rise from
a vomit launch pad, in loop de loops,
this is hard for me to say. And so, I
captain silence with an iceberg tongue.

And, as usual, I go along with Andre.
"It's going to be fun," he tells me, just
like he did when we used to
smack the asses of cars, to set off

their alarms when we were kids. And
it was fun, until Lucky Thompson's
father came out with his .44, cussing
holes in summer evening, aiming

at all creation. We had to hide for
twenty-seven days under Mr. Richards'
green Chevy Nova—or was it half an
hour? And later, was it an extension

cord or a telephone pole that Daddy
used to build us up on every leaning
side? Andre never cried, though we
were as guilty as roaches in the

refrigerator—not then, or in 2006,
when his right leg met a roadside
bomb in Iraq. He never cried when
nightmares came, and sleep became

a desert storming lead. Even after
years of underbelly unemployment,
he never loosed a sniffle. "Tears are
not the clothes of kings," he likes to

say—something that he read in a book,
I think, like he reads me now on these
rails. He tells me I should "man up,"
"get tough," steeple up my arms in air

of amusement squeals. And I do—as
I am used to doing, all except question
this man, who once would Spongebob
snot from my nose. But a week from

next Wednesday, when he jumps from
the roof of his 30 story life, and witnesses
say he sailed to earth without a sound,

I will wonder if tears finally came to

ride his cheeks down, just like we were
riding this coaster. I will wonder if he
closed his eyes to wipe them away, and
wish that I could catch that holy water.

On Fishing

It could be that we are standing
on the royal river Thames. It
could be that we are standing
on Potomac's go go shoals.
I might be Irish-French-Ghanaian.
You might be Asian-Sudanese.
We will not speak of this. We
will only speak of tackle boxes,
secret metal cities, mysteries
of hooks. Her body is too big
for us to be small, and she
reminds us here. It could be
I'm a biker-homosexual. You
might be ladies' man and priest.
We will not dwell on this. It
does not matter here. Her bottle
holds no gavels—no jury box
in waves. We will only speak
of casting—how every man's
line gets tangled—how many
have been cut. I will offer you
some bread, and you will eat.
You will offer me a beer and
I will drink. Laughter will
break like communion wafers.
This is all there is to say.

Summertime and the Living is DC

Congas cold cock hips
Cowbells empty clips
Horns take aim
Like Go Go troops
Chuck Brown bustin'
                    loose

Entitlement

(4 Alan King)

It's as if we're always on duty for them,
bellhops for Sisyphus, rickshaws without

the ricks, toilet paper carousels, forever
on call. King Alan tells me this tonight,

after a white man curses when he doesn't
hold the door for him at Mio's Restaurant

on Vermont Avenue in DC. He tells me this,
after a white man feels the punch of a pine

tree, and a plate glass window screams.
King Alan says, "I don't open doors for

white people anymore" — that, and "the
Handi Wipe has gone on strike."

The Holocaust Museum: June 10, 2009

(4 the late Stephen T. Johns)

First, they will say
it's all a lie.
Perhaps not tomorrow,
but one tomorrow coming,
they will call the .22
of my gunpowder plumes
nothing more
than jigglypuff clouds.
They will call my brass jacket,
my fedora of lead,
a fabricated fashion,
like they do that whole
Auschwitz-Birkenau,
gassing operations,
Einsatzgruppen,
Bergen-Belsen typhus,
ovens oiled with
Jewish bodies thing.
This will be the report
of dragon stooges,
even as their claws
help spark my primer flashes.

But the bottle always knows
the author of its breaking,
and so, if you weren't
already dead,
I'm sure that you'd
die laughing
at such denials
of all my point blank
penetrations—
you, your wife, your son,
die laughing—
sterben Sie lachend—
at all their hammer struck
head fakes,
practically split your sides
into 6 million pieces,
now that we've become
so close.

Epitaph for All

Where are the epitaphs for turtles,
funerals for swans?

Where are wakes for minnows,
eulogies for snails?

A rose was heard to raise these
questions, to a stunned

church of flowers at repast, how in
all their years covering

men's caskets, none of them
had ever thought to ask.

Rubber Side Up

A motorcycle fall
is a paramedic country,
filled with grave states,
CPR valleys.
(For an adult,
start with 15 compressions
2 rescue breaths.
1 & 2 & 3 &… One
lone State Trooper
is the first to arrive on scene.)
They will not
release your name
for days
or print news
of family.
But we will see you
on our way to grub
after Reverend Greene
has preached.
We will pass your
highway mattress,
your sticky tarmac pillow.
How quickly
do our lanes
slow to creeping.
How sudden
does the rubber stretch
of necks convene
to adjudicate your tossing.

Our eyes
comb hairlines
of freeway
to locate your renegade rocket.
But, it is hiding,
like your heartbeat.
What a parliament of sirens.
What a blitz of skid marks
stain this violated street.
(13 & 14 & 15 & breathe
& breathe) Waterfalls
of perspiration flow
from your policeman.
He is yours now.
You are each others.
Yet, only we
shall glimpse this—the face
of Maryland's finest
growing flushed,
the color of late June peonies.
After a dozen unrequited
kisses, the trooper's arms
cramp & shake.)
A motorcycle fall
is a stadium of ruptures,
a place where
fading plastic flowers
stake claims in urns
beside the roadway.
And for you—we will
come to find—
it is a plummet

from an on-ramp
into fast lane fathoms below.
It is death away
from quiet send offs,
balm of polished pews.
How dare you
force our containers
to stop and acknowledge
the denominator?
How dare you fill our eyes
with yellow tape,
your soaking
leather cloak of red?
We have already heard
one message today.
(At compression 152
help arrives & there is the
falling away of a trooper
like a wounded balloon,
or exhausted lover.
& there is the helicopter
that hovers,
& lands & freezes
the world
& lifts you up and up.
& there is the clap
of rotor blades
that cause us to cover
cans of ears
& there is rolling up
of windows
& finally traffic that budges,

after you are gone.)
But you were
already gone, weren't you,
like radials that
pancaked your stomach,
ribcage, spleen?
A motorcycle fall
is a sermon
to remember
on a pulpit where
no one ever
volunteers to preach.

Manor Care Midnight

(4 Joseph Larry Williams)

Watch what is left, the slurs and withered wicks
of weathered spines and razor wits. Watch them
if you can, as you're counting down the ticks.
Deny the guardrail beds, which stalk all men
and womenfolk, will rise. Pretend no ward
of drip-drawn bags will ever come to call.
Perhaps, even now, as you toast the charge
of years, I dare you to stop on by—walk
on by—the urine hellos that haunt these
halls. Deny the Lysol air, the puréed
stench will stymie you. Deny this faeces.
Believe you'll always stand, parade, through days.
No matter how bright you shine on the stage,
every light dims at the end of the play.

Thank you for buying **Bottle of Life**. Other books by Truth Thomas available under flipped eye publishing's imprints are **Party of Black** and **A Day of Presence**.

You can find more information on the author at:
http://truththomas.wordpress.com/

—§—

flipped eye publishing is dedicated to publishing powerful new voices in affordable volumes. Founded in 2001, we have won awards and international recognition through our focus on publishing fiction and poetry that is clear and true, rather than exhibitionist.

If you would like more information about flipped eye publishing, please join our mailing list online at **www.flippedeye.net**.

Lightning Source UK Ltd.
Milton Keynes UK
UKHW010719210321
380690UK00001B/50